Wilson

by Iain Gray

Lang**Syne**

PUBLISHING

WRITING *to* REMEMBER

79 Main Street, Newtongrange,
Midlothian EH22 4NA
Tel: 0131 344 0414
E-mail: info@lang-syne.co.uk
www.langsyneshop.co.uk

Design by Dorothy Meikle
Printed by Printwell Ltd
© Lang Syne Publishers Ltd 2023

All rights reserved. No part of this publication may be reproduced, stored or introduced into a retrieval system, or transmitted in any form or by any means (electronic, mechanical, photocopying, recording or otherwise) without the prior written permission of Lang Syne Publishers Ltd.

ISBN 978-1-85217-604-4

Wilson

MOTTOES include:
Deeds, rather than words
(and)
Always watchful
(and)
I will, who will not.

CRESTS include:
A demi-wolf rampant
(and)
A demi-lion rampant.

NAME variations include:
Willison
Willson
Willston

Chapter one:

The origins of popular surnames

by George Forbes and Iain Gray

***If you don't know where you came from, you won't know where you're going* is a frequently quoted observation and one that has a particular resonance today when there has been a marked upsurge in interest in genealogy, with increasing numbers of people curious to trace their family roots.**

Main sources for genealogical research include census returns and official records of births, marriages and deaths – and the key to unlocking the detail they contain is obviously a family surname, one that has been 'inherited' and passed from generation to generation.

No matter our station in life, we all have a surname – but it was not until about the middle of the fourteenth century that the practice of being identified by a particular surname became commonly established throughout the British Isles.

Previous to this, it was normal for a person to be identified through the use of only a forename.

But as population gradually increased and there were many more people with the same forename, surnames were adopted to distinguish one person, or community, from another.

Many common English surnames are patronymic in origin, meaning they stem from the forename of one's father – with 'Johnson,' for example, indicating 'son of John.'

It was the Normans, in the wake of their eleventh century conquest of Anglo-Saxon England, a pivotal moment in the nation's history, who first brought surnames into usage – although it was a gradual process.

For the Normans, these were names initially based on the title of their estates, local villages and chateaux in France to distinguish and identify these landholdings.

Such grand descriptions also helped enhance the prestige of these warlords and generally glorify their lofty positions high above the humble serfs slaving away below in the pecking order who had only single names, often with Biblical connotations as in Pierre and Jacques.

The only descriptive distinctions among the peasantry concerned their occupations, like 'Pierre the swineherd' or 'Jacques the ferryman.'

Roots of surnames that came into usage in England not only included Norman-French, but also Old French, Old Norse, Old English, Middle English, German, Latin, Greek, Hebrew and the Gaelic languages of the Celts.

The Normans themselves were originally Vikings, or 'Northmen', who raided, colonised and eventually settled down around the French coastline.

They had sailed up the Seine in their longboats in 900AD under their ferocious leader Rollo and ruled the roost in north eastern France before sailing over to conquer England in 1066 under Duke William of Normandy – better known to posterity as William the Conqueror, or King William I of England.

Granted lands in the newly-conquered England, some of their descendants later acquired territories in Wales, Scotland and Ireland – taking not only their own surnames, but also the practice of adopting a surname, with them.

But it was in England where Norman rule and custom first impacted, particularly in relation to the adoption of surnames.

This is reflected in the famous *Domesday Book*, a massive survey of much of England and Wales, ordered by William I, to determine who owned what, what it was worth and therefore how much they were liable to pay in taxes to the voracious Royal Exchequer.

Completed in 1086 and now held in the National Archives in Kew, London, 'Domesday' was an Old English word meaning 'Day of Judgement.'

This was because, in the words of one contemporary chronicler, "its decisions, like those of the Last Judgement, are unalterable."

It had been a requirement of all those English landholders – from the richest to the poorest – that they identify themselves for the purposes of the survey and for future reference by means of a surname.

This is why the *Domesday Book*, although written in Latin as was the practice for several centuries with both civic and ecclesiastical records, is an invaluable source for the early appearance of a wide range of English surnames.

Several of these names were coined in connection with occupations.

These include Baker and Smith, while Cooks, Chamberlains, Constables and Porters were to be found carrying out duties in large medieval households.

The church's influence can be found in names such as Bishop, Friar and Monk while the popular name of Bennett derives from the late fifth to mid-sixth century Saint Benedict, founder of the Benedictine order of monks.

The early medical profession is represented by Barber, while businessmen produced names that include Merchant and Sellers.

Down at the village watermill, the names that cropped up included Millar/Miller, Walker and Fuller, while other self-explanatory trades included Cooper, Tailor, Mason and Wright.

Even the scenery was utilised as in Moor, Hill, Wood and Forrest – while the hunt and the chase supplied names that include Hunter, Falconer, Fowler and Fox.

Colours are also a source of popular surnames, as in Black, Brown, Gray/Grey, Green and White, and would have denoted the colour of the clothing the person habitually wore or, apart from the obvious exception of 'Green', one's hair colouring or even complexion.

The surname Red developed into Reid, while

Blue was rare and no-one wanted to be associated with yellow.

Rather self-important individuals took surnames that include Goodman and Wiseman, while physical attributes crept into surnames such as Small and Little.

Many families proudly boast the heraldic device known as a Coat of Arms, as featured on our front cover.

The central motif of the Coat of Arms would originally have been what was borne on the shield of a warrior to distinguish himself from others on the battlefield.

Not featured on the Coat of Arms, but highlighted on page three, is the family motto and related crest – with the latter frequently different from the central motif.

Adding further variety to the rich cultural heritage that is represented by surnames is the appearance in recent times in lists of the 100 most common names found in England of ones that include Khan, Patel and Singh – names that have proud roots in the vast sub-continent of India.

Echoes of a far distant past can still be found in our surnames and they can be borne with pride in commemoration of our forebears.

Chapter two:

Born for battle

A name of truly martial roots, 'Wilson' derives from the personal name 'Will', a diminutive of 'William', which in turn stems from the Old German 'Willihelm', or 'Wilhelm.'

The name element 'will' is descriptive of dedication or fierce desire to emerge victorious from battle, while 'helm', means 'protection', such as that afforded by an armoured helmet.

Although, in common with many other surnames found in England today, it became popularised in the wake of the Norman Conquest of 1066, those who would come to bear it were present from much earlier times.

This means that flowing through the veins of many English bearers of the Wilson name today may well be the blood of those Germanic tribes who invaded and settled in the south and east of the island of Britain from about the early fifth century.

Known as the Anglo-Saxons, they were composed of the Jutes, from the area of the Jutland Peninsula in modern Denmark, the Saxons from

Lower Saxony, in modern Germany and the Angles from the Angeln area of Germany.

It was the Angles who gave the name 'Engla land', or 'Aengla land' – better known as 'England.'

They held sway in what became England from approximately 550 until the Norman Conquest of 1066, with the main kingdoms those of Sussex, Wessex, Northumbria, Mercia, Kent, East Anglia and Essex.

It was at the battle of Hastings in October of 1066 that Harold II, last of the Anglo-Saxon kings, was killed in the invasion led by Duke William of Normandy – with William later declared king and, within an astonishingly short space of time, Norman manners, customs and law imposed on England.

This laid the basis for what subsequently became established 'English' custom and practice.

The Wilson name, in the now redundant form of 'Willesen', first appears in the historical record in the early decades of the fourteenth century in Wakefield, Yorkshire, and it is with Yorkshire that early bearers of the name were particularly identified, although they were soon to be found throughout the length and breadth of the British Isles.

They figure prominently in the frequently turbulent historical record.

Born in about 1560 in Stamford, Lincolnshire, Sir Thomas Wilson was a leading government official, spy, author and translator.

Having studied civil law at Cambridge, he later received the patronage of Sir Robert Cecil, the spymaster to James I (James VI of Scotland), and who was later ennobled as Lord Salisbury.

On Cecil's behalf, Shaw travelled widely throughout the continent to gather intelligence on both Spanish and Papal plans against England.

Elected Member of Parliament (MP) for Newton, Isle of Wight, he later obtained the trusted post of Keeper of the Records at Whitehall Palace.

Knighted in 1618, he was one of the interrogators that year of the ill-fated courtier, colonial adventurer and prolific writer Sir Walter Raleigh and, after his execution he was given the responsibility of cataloguing his vast collection of books and papers; he died in 1629.

Rather less respectable than Shaw, Harriette Wilson, born in 1786, one of fifteen children, and whose father kept a small shop in London's fashionable Mayfair, was a celebrated Regency-era courtesan.

Beginning her 'career' when she was aged 15, among her famous clientele were William Craven, 1st Earl of Craven, and Arthur Wellesley, 1st Duke of Wellington.

When told that Harriette planned to write her decidedly steamy memoirs, the duke famously retorted: "Publish, and be damned!"

Her sisters Sophia, Fanny and Amy also became courtesans, with Sophia later attaining respectability when she married Lord Berwick.

Harriette Wilson died in 1845, while her memoirs, available today as *Publish and Be Damn'd: The Memoirs of Harriette Wilson*, were adapted for a BBC Radio 4 series in 2012.

On the battlefields of the First World War, Sir Henry Wilson, latest 1st Baronet of the name, was the senior British Army officer who served as commandant of the Staff College, Camberley and who, in 1918, was appointed Chief of the Imperial General Staff.

Born in 1864 at Currygrane, Co. Longford, Ireland, he was shot and killed on his doorstep by two IRA gunmen in April of 1922 after returning to his home from unveiling a war memorial at Liverpool Street railway station.

He was portrayed by Michael Redgrave in

the 1969 film *Oh! What a Lovely War* – a satire on military leadership during the First World War.

During the Second World War, Charles McMoran Wilson, born in 1882 in Skipton, Yorkshire was personal physician to British wartime leader Winston Churchill.

Author of *The Struggle for Survival*, about Churchill both during and after the war, he was elevated to the Peerage as 1st Baron Moran before his death in 1977, while he also served for a time as president of the Royal College of Physicians, London.

In the world of enterprise, James Wilson, born in 1805 in Hawick, in the Scottish Borders, the son of a wealthy textile mill owner, went on to found not only what is today's influential magazine *The Economist*, but also the Chartered Bank of India, Australia and China – which became Standard Chartered Bank in 1969 – while he also held high government office.

He moved to London with his older brother William when he was aged 19 and, funded by his father, opened a hat manufacturing business.

By the time he was aged 32, he had a net worth estimated at £25,000 – worth about £1.6m in today's terms.

In 1843, after having written on economic matters for a number of newspapers, he established *The Economist* as a newspaper to campaign for free trade, while in 1853 he founded what would later became Standard Chartered Bank.

For sixteen years the chief editor and sole proprietor of *The Economist* – which today, as a magazine, has a worldwide weekly circulation of 1.6 million – he later entered Parliament as Liberal MP for Westbury, Wiltshire.

Appointed Secretary of the Board of Control in 1848, between 1853 and 1858 he served as Financial Secretary to the Treasury.

Other posts held before his death in 1860 included Paymaster-General and Vice-President of the Board of Trade.

Chapter three:
Politics and the sciences

In twentieth century British politics, James Harold Wilson, better known as Harold Wilson and later more formally as Baron Wilson of Rievaulx, was the Labour Party politician who served from 1964 to 1970 and from 1974 to 1976 as Prime Minister.

Born in 1916 in Huddersfield, West Riding of Yorkshire, the son of a chemist and of a former schoolteacher, he was elected MP for Ormskirk in 1945 – and later Huyton, near Liverpool – posts he held before becoming Prime Minister included Secretary for Overseas development, President of the Board of Trade and Shadow Chancellor of the Exchequer.

With his 'trademark' pipe and Gannex raincoat, he became a familiar figure and was responsible for important legislation during his tenure as Prime Minister that includes the National Insurance Act of 1966.

In 1976, at the height of an economic crisis that had hit most Western nations, he suddenly announced his resignation as Prime Minister.

Created Baron Wilson of Rievaulx after standing down from the House of Commons in 1983, he died in 1995.

In 1999, a statue to him was unveiled by Labour Prime Minister Tony Blair outside Huddersfield railway station.

In his memoirs *Spycatcher: The Candid Autobiography of a Senior Intelligence Officer*, Peter Wright, a retired assistant director of the British intelligence agency MI5, controversially claimed that a cabal of disgruntled MI5 officers and others had acted together in an attempt to undermine Wilson while he was Prime Minister.

His widow, Gladys Mary Wilson (née Baldwin), Baroness Wilson of Rievaulx, born in 1916 in Diss, Norfolk, achieved her own personal fame with the publication in 1970 of her poetry collection *Selected Poems*.

Also in British Labour Party politics, Brian Wilson, born in 1948 in Dunoon, on the west coast of Scotland, held a number of top government posts that include, Minister of State and Energy Minister at the Department of Trade and Industry.

Along with three friends from Dundee University, in 1971 he established the weekly newspaper *The West Highland Free Press* on the Isle of Skye, while he is a director of Celtic Football Club – penning its official 1988 centenary history *Celtic, A Century with Honour*.

In American politics, Thomas Woodrow Wilson, better known as Woodrow Wilson, was the Democrat politician who served from 1913 to 1921 as 28th President of the United States

Born in 1856 in Staunton, Virginia, he played a leading role at the end of the First World War in promoting a League of Nations – in what sadly proved to be the forlorn hope that it would be instrumental in avoiding future conflicts; he died in 1924.

Bearers of the Wilson name have also stamped their mark in the sciences, with no fewer than two of the name receiving Nobel Prizes for their pioneering work.

Born in 1869 in Glencorse, Midlothian, Charles Thomas Rees was the Scottish physicist and meteorologist who received the Noble Prize in physics in 1927 for his invention, while working at Cambridge University, of the cloud chamber.

His work had involved expanding humid air within a sealed container and experimenting with the creation of cloud trails caused by ions and radiation.

A Fellow of the scientific think-tank the Royal Society, he died in 1959, while he gives his name to The Wilson Condensation Cloud formations that occur after very large explosions, and are now recognised as helping to explain the origins of the universe.

Another Nobel Prize winner in physics is the American astronomer Robert Woodrow Wilson, who shared the prize in 1978 along with Arno Allan Penzias for their discovery of cosmic microwave background radiation (CMB), which also contributes towards an understanding of the origins of the universe.

Born in 1936 in Houston, Texas, and also the recipient along with Penzias of the prestigious Henry Draper Medal of the National Academy of Sciences, he made the discovery while working at Bell Laboratories, New Jersey.

In the world of wildlife, Alexander Wilson was the Scots-born naturalist celebrated today as the "Father of American Ornithology."

Born in Paisley in 1779 and apprenticed for a time as a weaver, he incurred the wrath of the authorities after writing a satirical poem highlighting the dreadful working conditions in local mills.

Ordered to publicly burn what was perceived

as his seditious poem and sentenced to a brief period of imprisonment, he immigrated to America as a young man and settled at Gray's Ferry, Pennsylvania.

It was here that he met the naturalist William Bartram, who encouraged him in his interest in ornithology.

The result was that Wilson subsequently travelled widely throughout the United States cataloguing the nation's rich variety of bird life.

Complete with his own highly detailed drawings, his nine-volume *American Ornithology* was published between 1808 and 1814.

He died in 1813, a year before the publication of the final volume, while a number of species of North American bird – including Wilson's plover, Wilson's snipe and Wilson's storm-petrel are named for him.

There is a statue to him in the grounds of the abbey in his home town of Paisley, while the *Wilson Ornithological Society* and the *Wilson Journal of Ornithology* bear his name.

One particularly infamous bearer of the otherwise proud name of Wilson was the career criminal and member of the Great Train Robbery gang Charlie Wilson.

Born in 1930 in Battersea, London, he was one of the gang of 17 who in August of 1963 robbed £2.6m – the equivalent of approximately £46m today – from a Royal Mail train that had been travelling between Glasgow and London, with the robbery taking place at Bridego Railway Bridge, near Mentmore, Buckinghamshire.

As the gang's 'treasurer', Wilson was responsible for handing out their individual shares of the ill-gotten gains.

He was quickly captured and jailed for 30 years, but managed to break out of Winson Green Prison, Birmingham, in August of 1964 – only four months into his sentence.

Fleeing to Canada with his family and settling in Rigaud, Quebec and later in the South of France, he was eventually recaptured in January of 1968 – finally emerging from prison more than ten years later.

Moving to Marbella, Spain, and thought to have been involved in drug smuggling, he was shot by an unknown gunman at the front door of his hacienda in April of 1990.

The killer has never been caught, but the murder is thought to have been as a result of his involvement in the robbery in November of 1983 of three tonnes of gold bullion and £26m worth of cash and diamonds from a warehouse at Heathrow Airport, London, belonging to the security and protection company Brink's-MAT.

Tasked with laundering some of the proceeds, Wilson lost the 'investors' £3m – and this has been seen as a possible motive for his as yet unsolved murder.

Chapter four:

On the world stage

Ranked as one of popular music's most influential and creative figures, Brian Wilson, born in 1942 in Inglewood, California, is the founder member of the band the Beach Boys.

It was along with his brothers Dennis, born in 1944 and who died in 1983, Carl, born in 1946 and who died in 1998, cousin Mike Love and Al Jardine that he formed the band – enjoying early chart success with singles that include the 1963 *Surfin' USA*.

Later hits include *Sloop John B.*, *Help Me, Rhonda* and the classic *Good Vibrations*, while their 1966 album *Pet Sounds* – composed and produced by Brian Wilson – is rated as one of the greatest of all time.

Other top albums include *Smile*, while Wilson, who at the height of his fame suffered from alcohol and drug problems, is an inductee of the Rock and Roll Hall of Fame.

A biopic on his life, *Love and Mercy*, is scheduled for release in 2014.

Through his marriage to Marilyn Rovell, a

singer with the band the Honeys, he is the father of the singer **Carnie Wilson**.

Born in 1968, along with her younger sister Wendy and Chynna Phillips, daughter of John and Michelle Phillips of the Mamas and Papas fame, she formed the band Wilson Phillips.

Born in 1944 in Greenville, Mississippi, **Mary Wilson** is the American singer who in 1961 formed the band the Primettes, later to gain international fame after they changed their name to the Supremes.

Major hits include *When the Lovelight Starts Shining Through His Eyes*, *Where Did Our Love Go*, *Up the Ladder to the Roof* and *Stoned Love*, while the band – at one stage renamed Diana Ross and the Supremes – are the recipient of a star on the Hollywood Walk of Fame.

Wilson's autobiography, *Dreamgirl: My Life as a Supreme*, was published in 1986.

Also the recipient of a star on the Hollywood Walk of Fame, **Nancy Wilson** is the American jazz, blues, pop and cabaret singer and actress born in 1937 in Chillicothe, Ohio, the daughter of an iron foundry worker and a domestic servant.

Major hits she has enjoyed include her 1960

debut single *Guess Who I Saw Today*, the 1963 *Tell Me the Truth* and, from 1968, *Face It Girl, It's Over*.

A leading celebrity light of America's civil rights movement in the 1960s, she is an inductee of the International Civil Rights Walk of Fame at the Martin Luther King, Jr., National Historic Site in Atlanta, Georgia, and also an inductee of the Big Band and Jazz Hall of Fame.

Dubbed "Mr Excitement" and "The Black Elvis", Jack Leroy Wilson, Jr., was the American rhythm and blues and soul star better known as **Jackie Wilson**.

Born in 1934 in Detroit, he became famed for hits that include his 1957 *Reet Petite (The Finest Girl You Ever Want to Meet)* and the 1961 *I'm Comin' Back to You*.

He was also famed for his electrifying stage performance that according to one account involved 'knee drops, splits, spins, one-footed across-the-floor slides, removing his tie and jacket on-stage and throwing it off-stage, and a lot of basic boxing steps – advance and retreat shuffling.'

An inductee of the Rock and Roll Hall of Fame and ranked at 69th in *Rolling Stone* magazine's list of the 100 Greatest Artists of All Time, he died in

1984. After collapsing from a heart attack on stage in 1975 he lapsed into a coma that persisted for nine years.

On British shores, **Paul "Pablo" Wilson**, born in 1978 in Kinlochleven, is the Scottish guitarist for the band Snow Patrol, while **Barrie Wilson**, born in 1947 in London and who died in 1990, was the English rock drummer with the band Procol Harum, best known for their iconic 1967 hit *A Whiter Shade of Pale*.

Born in 1978 in Keighley, West Yorkshire, Charles Richard Wilson, better known as **Ricky Wilson**, is the lead singer of the band the Kaiser Chiefs, whose hits include *I Predict a Riot*, *Oh My God* and *Everyday I Love You Less and Less*.

In 2013 he was appointed one of the mentors for acts on the television musical popularity contest *The Voice UK*.

Listed by *Hit Parader* magazine as one of the best female vocalists in rock music history, **Ann Wilson** is lead singer and songwriter with the American band Heart.

Born in 1950 in San Diego, California, she founded the band in 1974 along with her younger sister Nancy Wilson, born in 1954.

Album success they have enjoyed include the 1978 album *Dog and Butterfly*, while Ann Wilson also had a hit, along with Mike Reno, with the single *Almost Paradise*, featured in the 1984 film *Footloose*.

Known as "Mr Manchester", Anthony Howard Wilson, better known as **Tony Wilson**, was the radio and television presenter who, along with Alan Erasmus, founded the Manchester-based record label Factory records in 1978, signing up bands that include Joy Division, New Order, Orchestral Manoeuvres in the Dark and Happy Mondays.

Born in 1950 and a former presenter of the Granada Television programme *The Other Side of Midnight*, he died in 2007.

From music to the highly competitive world of sport, John Thomas Wilson, better known as **Jocky Wilson**, was the Scottish darts player who won the Professional Darts Championship in both 1982 and 1989.

Born in 1950 in Fife and spending much of his early life in an orphanage, it was after a succession of jobs that included coal delivery driver and miner in Seafield Colliery, Kirkcaldy, that in 1979 he took up darts as a profession after winning a darts competition at an Ayrshire holiday camp.

Cursed with an unfortunate relationship with alcohol, the nevertheless talented player died, a virtual recluse, in 2012.

Following his darts win in 1982 Wilson, fond of not only alcohol but also tobacco and sweets, decided to invest £1,200 of his winnings in a new set of dentures. He rarely wore them, however, claiming that they 'made him belch while drinking.'

In the world of contemporary darts, **James Wilson**, born in Huddersfield in 1972, is the English player who in 2012 was ranked 4th in the world.

On the fields of European football, Robert Primrose Wilson, born of Scots parentage in Chesterfield in 1943 and better known as **Bob Wilson**, is the former Scotland international goal keeper who played for teams that include Nottingham Forest and Arsenal and, after retiring from the game, went on to a successful career as a respected radio and television football pundit.

He is also noted as the founder in 1999, along with his wife Meg, of the national charity The Willow Foundation.

Established as a memorial to their daughter Anna, who died of cancer when she was aged 31, it provides support for seriously ill 16 to 40-year-olds.

From sport to the stage, **Fiona Mary Wilson**, born in Co. Cork in 1958, is the Irish actress better known by her married name of **Fiona Shaw**.

Known for her role of Petunia Dursley, Harry Potter's aunt in the *Harry Potter* series of films, she is also an acclaimed stage actress – winning the Laurence Olivier Award for Best Actress for her performance in the 1993 production of *Machinal*.

Also the winner of the 1996 Drama Desk Award for Outstanding One-Person-Show for her performance in *The Waste Land* at New York's Liberty Theatre, her other screen credits include the 1989 *My Left Foot* and the 1995 *Persuasion*.

One of an American acting dynasty, **Andrew Wilson** is the actor and film director born in 1964.

His screen credits include the 1996 *Bottle Rocket* and the 2001 *Zoolander*, while he is the brother of fellow actors **Owen** and **Luke Wilson**.

Born in 1968, Owen is the star of films that include the 2001 *The Royal Tenenbaums* and the 2006 *Night at the Museum*, while his brother Luke also appeared in *The Royal Tenenbaums* and the 2001 *Legally Blonde*.

Born in Los Angeles in 1987, **Mara Wilson** is the American actress best known for her role, as a child actress, of Matilda in the 1996 film of the same name and that of Nattie Hillard in the 1993 *Mrs Doubtfire*.

On British television screens, **Richard Wilson**, born in Greenock in 1936, is the Scottish actor best known for his role of Victor Meldrew in the popular British sitcom *One Foot in the Grave*; also an accomplished stage actor, he is the recipient of an OBE.

Born in 1982 in Ashford, Surrey, **Ruth Wilson** is the English actress best known for big screen credits that include the 2005 *Suburban Shootout*, the 2006 television drama *Jane Eyre*, for which she won a BAFTA and a Golden Globe Award nomination for Best Actress in a mini-series, and the 2010 crime drama *Luther*.

Behind the camera lens, **Andy Wilson**, born in 1958, is the British theatre, film and television director with directing credits for television that include *Psychos*, *Spooks*, *Hotel Babylon* and *Ripper Street*.

Born in London in 1939, **Ian Wilson** is the British cinematographer whose credits include *The Flame Trees of Thika*, for which he won a BAFTA Award nomination in 1982, the 1992 *The Crying*

Game and, from 1999, *A Christmas Carol*, for which he received an Emmy Award nomination.

Bearers of the Wilson name have also achieved fame in the creative world of the written word.

Born in 1945 in Bath, Somerset, **Jacqueline Wilson**, more formally known as Dame Jacqueline Wilson, is the author of the highly successful *Tracy Beaker* series of children's novels, several of which have been adapted for television.

British Children's Laureate from 2005 to 2007, her many literary awards include a *Guardian* Children's Fiction Prize and, for her 2002 *The Story of Tracy Beaker*, the Blue Peter People's Choice Award.

Born in 1950, Andrew Norman Wilson is the author, journalist and newspaper columnist better known as **A.N. Wilson**; his book on Leo Tolstoy won the Whitbread Award for Best Biography in 1988, while his 2007 novel *Winnie and Wolf* was long-listed for the Man Booker Prize.

Also in the world of journalism, Charles Wilson, better known as **Charlie Wilson**, is the Scottish newspaper executive born in Glasgow in 1940.

A former member of the Royal Marines, where he became a boxing champion, he served as editor of *The Times* from 1985 to 1990 and, from 1995 to 1996, *The Independent*.

Previously having edited the *Glasgow Evening Times*, the former *Scottish Sunday Standard* and the *Herald*, he was married for a time to the journalist and television broadcaster Anne Robinson, before marrying the journalist Sally O'Sullivan.

Famed as the author of the novel *A Clockwork Orange*, adapted for a film of the same name by director Stanley Kubrick in 1971, John Anthony Burgess Wilson was the author better known by his pen name of **Anthony Burgess**.

Born in Manchester in 1917 and a Fellow of the Royal Society of Literature, he died in 1993.